Contents

Cannabis – what's the deal? . . . . .

The cannabis plant 6

Different forms 8

What does cannabis do? 10

Who takes cannabis? 14

Why do people take cannabis? 16

Short-term effects 18

Getting hooked? 22

Giving up 24

Long-term effects 26

Losing out 30

Serious consequences 32

A gateway drug? 34

An ancient cure 36

The cannabis business 38

Cannabis and the law 42

Should the law be changed? 46

Cannabis and schools 48

Help and advice 50

Glossary 52

Contacts and further information 54

Index 56

▌Words appearing in the text in bold, **like this**, are explained in the Glossary.

Cannabis – what's the deal?

Ben first tried smoking cannabis when he was fourteen – just to see how it felt. He was soon taking every chance he could to get high.

Soon, Ben began to have serious problems at school. Most mornings he had to drag himself out of bed, still feeling **stoned** from the night before. When he wasn't high he was arguing with his girlfriend, who hated the way he was always so "out of it". Within a few months, he had split up from his girlfriend and was spending most of his time smoking cannabis alone.

Ben realized that his parents were worried sick about him – and to make things even worse he'd started stealing from his mother to pay for more cannabis. He knew that his life was falling apart, but he couldn't seem to do anything about it. He just kept on smoking to help him forget his problems.

The crunch came when Ben was caught smoking cannabis at school. He was told that he could be expelled – just before some important exams – and everyone was very angry and upset. Ben was forced to take a long, hard look at his life. Was he really going to throw everything away, just for the sake of smoking cannabis?

Do you think that you might find yourself in Ben's situation? Every year, thousands of teenagers find that smoking cannabis has taken over their lives – and if you make the wrong decisions it could be you.

Making decisions

This book has the information you need to help you make your own decisions about cannabis. It looks at the ways people use the drug and what it does to their bodies and minds. It examines whether cannabis is a "**gateway drug**" that can lead on to hard drugs such as heroin, and it considers the link between smoking cannabis and serious mental illness.

There are also wider issues to think about. How do the powerful **drug barons** control the cannabis trade? What have different governments done to tackle the problem, and is there a case for making cannabis legal? Get ready to find out – what's the deal with cannabis?

❚ Most people who smoke cannabis never stop to think about the serious effects the drug can have on their bodies and their minds.

The cannabis plant

The leafy cannabis plant has been grown for thousands of years in warm, sunny parts of the world. Cannabis stems can be made into useful products, such as rope and cloth. However, its leaves and flowers are often put to a very different use. They can be used to produce an **intoxicating** drug.

Using the stems

As early as the first century BC, people in China were using the stems of the cannabis plant to produce **hemp**. Hemp is a strong, stringy fibre that can be made into ropes, rough cloth, and even paper. People in ancient China used it mainly for making nets and mats.

⚠ Two types of cannabis

There are two main types (or species) of cannabis plant. The stems of the tall *Cannabis sativa* plant are used for producing hemp, while its leaves and flowers are used to make the cannabis drug. The smaller and bushier *Cannabis indica* has darker leaves and a strong musky smell. It is used purely for producing the cannabis drug.

During the time of the Roman Empire, cannabis was grown in many parts of Asia. The Romans needed hemp to make ropes and sails for their sailing ships, and they started growing cannabis in Europe also. In the nineteenth century, the age of the great sailing ships, cannabis was widely cultivated. At this time, the plant was introduced into the southern United States, where it soon spread widely as a weed.

Other uses

At the same time as people in ancient China were discovering the useful properties of cannabis stems, they were also finding other uses for the plant. The Chinese found that they could produce a soothing oil from cannabis seeds that helped to dull the pain of cramps and fevers. Very early on, people also discovered that they could get intoxicated, or **high**, by smoking the plant's flowers and leaves.

By the twentieth century, most ships were driven by steam. This meant there was much less demand for hemp. In most parts of the world, people stopped growing the cannabis plant for its stems. Instead, many growers turned their attention to producing the plant's flowers and leaves. Around this time, governments started to become aware of the dangerous effects of smoking cannabis. They began to take measures to make the drug illegal. However, a worldwide business of drug producing had already begun.

I Cannabis is grown in many parts of the world, but especially in countries that have a warm and sunny climate, such as China, Colombia, Thailand, and Nigeria.

Different forms

Cannabis is sold in several different forms. The most common type is **leaf cannabis**, but it is also available as blocks of **resin**, and as an oil. Strengths of the drug vary, and in recent years some very strong forms of cannabis have made their way on to the streets.

Leaf cannabis

Leaf cannabis is a mixture of dried leaves and flowering heads. Commonly known as "grass" or "weed", it is often mixed with tobacco and smoked in a **joint** (a hand-made cigarette). Leaf cannabis is sometimes smoked in a pipe, or in a **bong** – a kind of water pipe. In recent years, some people have begun to smoke cannabis in blunts. These are cigars that have been opened up, emptied of tobacco, and then re-filled with cannabis.

Getting stronger

During the 1970s, most users smoked leaf cannabis made from the *Cannabis sativa* plant (see page 6). Today, however, cannabis sold on the streets often comes from the *Cannabis indica* plant. Known as "skunk" because it has an unpleasant smell, it is much stronger than cannabis from the *Cannabis sativa* plant and makes users much sleepier and more groggy.

▌ The practice of using a bong, or water pipe, first began in Asia.

I The most common method of smoking cannabis is in a hand-made cigarette.

Hashish

Hashish (or **hash**) is made from the sap of the cannabis plant. This sap hardens to form a resin, which can be made into sticky balls, chunks, or flakes. Like leaf cannabis, hash is often mixed with tobacco and smoked in a joint or a pipe. It can be much stronger than weaker forms of leaf cannabis. It also carries extra dangers because **dealers** mix it with other substances, such as paper pulp, in order to bulk it out and make more profit.

Hashish can be boiled in a **solvent** such as alcohol to produce a very potent (strong) oil. This oil is usually mixed with tobacco or leaf cannabis, but sometimes it is smoked on its own in a water pipe. Hash oil can be more than ten times as strong as leaf cannabis, and users may experience some very frightening effects.

Cooking with cannabis

Sometimes people add cannabis to foods such as biscuits, brownies, or cake. This can be very risky. It is hard to judge the strength of cannabis when it is taken in this way. The drug also takes longer to have an effect, so it's easy to take dangerous amounts.

! Different names

Cannabis is known by many names. Some of its common names are marijuana, grass, pot, ganja, dope, weed, skunk, and herb. Cannabis cigarettes, or joints, are also known as **spliffs** or reefers.

9

What does cannabis do?

Did you know that cannabis contains over 400 chemicals? Some have a powerful effect on the brain, changing the way people think and behave. The effects of cannabis vary greatly. Some people feel very ill the first time they try the drug, while others hardly notice any changes, and certainly don't feel **high**. But most users agree that there are certain stages that they usually go through when they smoke cannabis.

A powerful chemical

The most powerful chemical in the cannabis plant is called delta-9-tetrahydrocannabinol – or **THC** for short. It is found in its most **concentrated** form in cannabis flowers, but it is also found in a weaker form in the plant's leaves.

When someone smokes cannabis, THC travels through their lungs and into their bloodstream. Then it is carried around the body, reaching the heart and brain. Very soon, the heart begins to race. Cannabis users also experience a high as the THC gets to work on their brain.

Inside the brain

Once it reaches the brain, THC reacts with special **receptors**. These receptors respond to the chemical's stimulus and send messages throughout the body. The messages tell the body to relax. They also heighten the senses, such as sight and taste.

THC has the effect of exaggerating people's moods. If someone is feeling happy and relaxed when they take cannabis, the drug can make them feel happier. This feeling of happiness, combined with the heightening of the senses, causes the user to feel high.

Question

How long does it take for cannabis to affect the brain?

However, THC also has the effect of strengthening negative feelings, such as depression or fear. When this happens the user does not feel high, but instead experiences feelings of panic and anxiety (see pages 20–21).

Acting on memory

One of the parts of the brain where THC takes effect is the *hippocampus* – the area where memories are formed. Research has shown that taking cannabis can seriously affect a person's short-term memory. After smoking cannabis, people often forget for a while exactly where they are, and what they had planned to do next.

Other effects

As well as its **intoxicating** effects, cannabis has other effects on the body. Research has shown that cannabis smoke contains higher concentrations of cancer-causing chemicals than tobacco smoke. If cannabis is smoked with tobacco, the dangers to health are even greater. (You can read more about these risks on page 26–27.)

▍Smoking cannabis can make people feel cut off from everything around them.

Answer

If cannabis is smoked, the effects begin within minutes. If it is eaten, it can take over an hour before the user starts to feel high.

11

I When the munchies take effect, people can consume vast quantities of food.

Getting stoned

The effects of cannabis vary according to a person's mood, but most cannabis users describe a sensation of getting **high** or "out of it" as the drug first starts to work on their brain and body. They experience a sense of relaxation and find that sights, sounds, and tastes seem more vivid. They also lose their sense of reality, becoming vague and "spaced out".

While people are high on cannabis they find it hard to complete thoughts and sentences, or to take in any new information. They also lose track of time. For people under the influence of cannabis, quite brief events can seem to stretch out for ages and fairly simple tasks can take a very long time to complete.

Question

How can someone tell what effects cannabis will have on them?

I After an evening of smoking cannabis, it's very hard to get up the following morning.

Changing the mood

As well as being "spaced out", cannabis users may experience a change of mood. Many people report that the drug makes them feel happy. While they are high, they may find things hilarious that they would normally find only slightly funny.

However, other people experience a less enjoyable change of mood. They may become withdrawn and depressed when they take cannabis. Some people also become very anxious or **paranoid**.

The munchies

After two or three hours, the effects of the drug gradually wear off. At this stage, cannabis users usually become extremely hungry. This sensation – known as the **munchies** – can lead cannabis users to eat very large amounts, and people often gorge themselves on junk food.

The morning after

Cannabis stays in the body for at least 36 hours, so users are still affected by the drug the following day. The after-effects of cannabis can leave people groggy and confused the following morning. They usually also feel irritable and low.

!Scary mixtures

Some people mix cannabis with alcohol or other drugs. This can have some very frightening results. In particular, when cannabis is mixed with alcohol, both drugs have a stronger effect. Taking a mixture of cannabis and alcohol often leads to vomiting, dizziness, and **panic attacks**.

Answer

It's impossible to know. But cannabis has the effect of heightening people's moods, so if someone has a tendency to be depressed or anxious, cannabis will usually increase this tendency.

Who takes cannabis?

What sort of people take cannabis? The answer is – all sorts. Some take the drug on a regular basis, while many others only smoke cannabis occasionally. Members of the **Rastafarian** religion smoke the drug as part of their religious ceremonies. There are also some people who use cannabis to help them deal with painful medical conditions.

A hippy drug

In Western countries, people first started smoking cannabis around the beginning of the twentieth century, but it didn't become widespread until the 1960s, when the **hippy** movement began. Then, smoking cannabis and eating **hash** cakes became very popular among young people.

While most hippies stopped taking cannabis as they got older, a few continued to use the drug. Many of today's older cannabis users first started smoking the drug in the 1960s.

I During the 1960s, smoking cannabis was often part of a hippy lifestyle.

Teenage trends

In the 1990s, teenage use of cannabis increased. Before that, it was mainly taken by adults. Today, there is evidence that some very young teenagers are smoking cannabis. However, the vast majority of young people do not use cannabis. Indeed, some research suggests that cannabis use among teenagers may have fallen in the last few years.

Rastafarians

Rastafarianism is a religion that began in Jamaica in the 1930s. For the Rastafarians, smoking cannabis is part of their religion. However, their religion does not suggest that cannabis should be smoked outside of their religious ceremonies. Rastafarians also have very clear rules about avoiding alcohol and coffee.

Seeking relief

Some people with certain medical conditions say that cannabis provides them with welcome pain relief. They claim that the drug reduces the symptoms of **multiple sclerosis** and **Parkinson's disease** (see pages 36–37). Some people who suffer from these illnesses say that they don't take cannabis in order to get **high**. They simply use the drug to make their lives more bearable.

▌Many Rastafarians smoke cannabis, which they call "ganja", as part of a religious experience.

❗ Young cannabis users

A recent survey in the United States revealed that between 1991 and 2001, the number of eighth graders (aged thirteen to fourteen) who had tried cannabis doubled from one in ten to one in five. However, the number of cannabis users in this age group has fallen in the last few years.

Why do people take cannabis?

Cannabis is the world's most widely taken illegal drug, and its use is growing fast. Why do so many people take up smoking cannabis?

I In the 1970s, the Rastafarian musician Bob Marley helped to make cannabis seem cool. Many of his songs are about cannabis and he was often photographed smoking a **joint**.

Being cool?

Many people think that taking cannabis is a cool thing to do. They hear about famous figures smoking the drug and think that it looks glamorous and fun. But for many celebrities, smoking cannabis has put their careers in danger. Some really talented football stars and athletes have been dropped from teams or disqualified from vital competitions because of their cannabis habit. Many rock musicians have admitted that smoking too much cannabis has robbed them of the energy and drive they needed to really make it big.

Out to shock

For many young people, one of the main attractions of taking cannabis is the sense of doing something rebellious and shocking. They start smoking cannabis to show the world that they're different – and that they don't care about the rules. But being a rebel doesn't always feel good. Can you imagine how it would feel to end up with a massive fine or even a stretch in jail?

Part of the gang

Some young people may try cannabis because they feel under pressure from their friends. They may be at a party where cannabis is being passed around. They may think that if they don't join in with the group, they will start to lose their friends. In this situation, the pressure someone can feel may not come from what their friends are saying, but it certainly comes from what they are doing.

What's important to remember is that everyone should be free to make their own decisions. Real friends accept you as you are.

Pressure from dealers

Many young people face the experience of being offered cannabis by a **dealer**. This may happen on the street, at a party, or in a nightclub. The dealer may even be a contact of a friend. Often, cannabis dealers can be very friendly and persuasive. In situations like this, the best thing to do is simply but firmly say no. If a dealer sees that you are not interested they will usually stop bothering you.

Chilling out?

Many people say that they smoke cannabis to escape from the stresses and worries of life. They say it makes them feel "chilled out", so nothing seems to matter very much any more. But chilling out doesn't make worries go away. In fact, most problems get worse if people escape into a daze instead of working out how to make things better.

▌ It's not easy to stick up for yourself and be different – but you're the only one who knows what's right for you.

Short-term effects

Cannabis has a number of physical and mental effects on its users. Some of these only take place while the user is **high**, but others may last for longer. Because cannabis stays in the body for 36 hours or more, many regular users are never completely free of its effects.

Physical effects

The physical effects of taking cannabis leave most people with bloodshot eyes and a dry mouth and throat. While they are high, people's reactions slow right down, and they move and talk much more slowly than usual. Under the influence of cannabis, physical movements become clumsy and **uncoordinated**, and concentration is also badly affected. These effects make it extremely dangerous for people to perform complex actions such as riding a bike or driving a car.

❙ Driving while under the influence of cannabis can have fatal results – not only for the cannabis user, but also for their friends and other innocent people.

Jake's story

People under the influence of cannabis have problems judging distances and reacting to signals and sounds. This makes driving very dangerous indeed. This is what happened to Jake, a college student, and his friends.

*"One night, after we'd had a few **spliffs**, we all decided it would be fun to go for a drive. Everyone was laughing and out of it – including me. I only realized when I started to drive just how **stoned** I was. I couldn't focus properly, and lights kept coming at me from nowhere. I swerved right off the road and crashed into a tree. We ended up with bruises – and a wrecked car – but at least we were alive. I still have nightmares about that night."*

▮ When a young person loses their ability to concentrate and take in information, they are putting their future at risk.

Mental effects

Cannabis also has a powerful impact on thinking, stopping the memory from functioning properly, and affecting people's judgement. While they are high, people often make choices they wouldn't normally make. They also lose their **inhibitions**, so they take greater risks than usual. All of these effects can lead people to make some bad mistakes, such as having unprotected sex, which they later regret.

What about the next day?

Cannabis stays in the body for a surprisingly long time. Even after a one-off use, traces of the drug can be detected in the body for three to five days. This means that most cannabis users are still experiencing the drug's effects the following day. Most of them feel sluggish and **lethargic**, and they also find it very hard to concentrate.

These effects on thinking are extremely worrying in the case of young people. Many young cannabis smokers arrive at school or college, still suffering from the effects of the cannabis they smoked the night before. This makes them unable to take in properly what they are being taught.

■ Cannabis can have some frightening effects. Many cannabis users have reported panic attacks.

Question

What do you do if someone you are with becomes paranoid after taking cannabis?

Everyone's out to get me

Sooner or later most cannabis takers have a bad experience, when instead of feeling happy and relaxed they feel anxious and jumpy. This frightening experience is sometimes known as **cannabis psychosis**. Feelings of anxiety and panic are especially common among inexperienced cannabis users, but longer-term users also experience **panic attacks** if they have taken a larger than usual amount of the drug, or a stronger, more **concentrated** dose.

Some cannabis users describe a range of **paranoid** symptoms, from feeling anxious, restless, and irritable, to serious panic attacks, when their heart races uncontrollably and they feel clammy and sick. Sometimes people believe that all their friends are turning against them – laughing at them and saying nasty things behind their backs. Others describe being too scared to walk along a street at night – and feeling convinced that someone will jump out and attack them. Symptoms like these can be very frightening.

"I'd tried smoking weed a few times before, but nothing prepared me for this. I felt like I was on the run from something really horrible – my heart just wouldn't stop thumping, and I felt dizzy and sick. I buried my head in my boyfriend's shoulder and stayed there for hours – just longing to feel normal again."

Laura, a teenager who "spun out" after taking a strong dose of cannabis

Spinning out

Another unpleasant **side effect** of cannabis is a feeling of dizziness and nausea. First-time users often feel sick and may vomit, while more experienced users suffer similar symptoms when they have taken too much of the drug.

Cannabis users describe feeling intensely sick, dizzy, and "out of it". These frightening sensations are often described as "spinning out". Like people who have drunk too much alcohol, they often vomit, but this doesn't make them feel any better. The only way to recover is simply to wait until the effects eventually become weaker.

Answer

Stay with them and reassure them. Try to keep them calm and let them know that everything will be all right. The symptoms of paranoia will slowly disappear. However, if they continue, you should contact a doctor.

Getting hooked?

Cannabis does not appear to cause physical **addiction** in the same way as many other drugs. But this doesn't mean it is easy to give up. The main problem with cannabis is **psychological dependence**. Many cannabis users start to rely on the feelings that the drug gives them, simply in order to cope with their lives. For thousands of cannabis users, cannabis dependence is a serious problem.

⚠ Cannabis dependence

According to the US National Institute on Drug Abuse, cannabis dependence is a serious problem, mainly because the drug is so widely used. More young people seek treatment for cannabis dependence than for all other illegal drugs combined.

Physical tolerance

When a drug is physically addictive, it causes changes in the user's body, which make their body need the drug in order to function. This is what happens when people become addicted to tobacco. The same effect does not appear to happen with cannabis. However, cannabis does have some serious physical effects.

A person who smokes cannabis every day builds up a **tolerance** to the drug, as their body requires larger and larger doses in order to experience the same effects. To get the same effects as an occasional user, a heavy user may need a dose that is as much as eight times higher. This means that the level of the drug in their body remains very high. It also means that they are at serious risk from all the negative health effects of cannabis described on pages 26–29.

Psychological dependence

The main problem with regular cannabis use is the user's psychological dependence on the drug. With regular use, heavy cannabis users begin to **crave** the feelings of relaxation that cannabis gives them, and feel bad when they can't have them. They lose the ability to feel calm or happy without the help of cannabis, and become dependent on the drug.

Question

What is psychological dependence?

▌Heavy cannabis users may experience strong feelings of depression if they are unable to get a dose of their drug.

The nicotine hook

When cannabis smokers mix their drug with tobacco, they soon become addicted to **nicotine**. The nicotine in tobacco very quickly leads to physical addiction and cravings. Often, people are introduced to tobacco through smoking cannabis. Many of these people end up with a serious smoking habit – even if they decide to give up smoking cannabis.

Answer

When someone is psychologically dependent on a drug, they rely on that drug because of the way it affects their emotions and their moods.

Giving up

There are many reasons why people decide to give up cannabis. Some cannabis users simply make the decision to stop completely, while others take a more gradual approach.

> "Since I've given up weed, I've had more energy. I'm able to get up early in the morning and I'm thinking much more clearly."
>
> Alice, a college student, who decided to quit smoking cannabis

Wake-up calls

For some long-term users, the cannabis experience can suddenly turn bad. Instead of experiencing a **high** when they light up, they find they are repeatedly plunged into sweats and panics. Most cannabis users experience an occasional **paranoid** reaction, especially if they take large quantities of the drug, but some users suddenly start to react like this every time they smoke a **joint**. Nobody knows why people start to get these reactions, but they usually cause users to stop smoking cannabis.

Deciding to quit

Sometimes people make a definite decision to stop taking cannabis. They may be worried about the damage to their health, or the effect that it's having on their thinking. They may be starting a new relationship, and feel that they don't need to take drugs any more. Or they may have some important exams coming up and want to be on top form. Whatever the reason, they come to the same decision – to take complete charge of their life again.

❗ Finding help

Not everyone finds it easy to give up cannabis, but there is help available. The organization Marijuana Anonymous has a twelve-step programme to help people quit (see pages 54–55).

Stopping gradually

For others, giving up cannabis is a more gradual process. They may stop hanging around with their old group of friends, or they may be starting on a new stage of their lives. In cases like this, people often find that they are simply smoking cannabis less and less often. Many people find that after a while they simply don't want to take cannabis any more.

Withdrawal symptoms

For people who do not use cannabis heavily, there are no noticeable **withdrawal symptoms** when they stop taking the drug. However, heavy users, whose bodies have become used to large quantities of cannabis, may experience some unpleasant effects. Once they stop taking cannabis they may feel sweaty, sick, and irritable. They may have difficulty sleeping and have intense and frightening dreams. These withdrawal symptoms are unpleasant, but they usually only last for two to four days.

▌ When people give up cannabis they are often surprised at how much more enjoyment they get out of life and how much more energy they have.

Long-term effects

For long-term users of cannabis, there are a number of worrying effects. These can range from a general lack of energy to extremely serious health problems. Many long-term cannabis users also suffer from poor concentration and memory loss. For some people, the consequences are even worse. Cannabis use has been linked to some very serious mental illnesses.

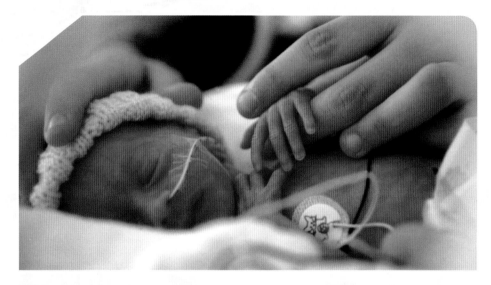

▌Heavy cannabis smokers can give birth to very small babies, who need special care in order to survive.

Smoking damage

For almost all cannabis users, taking cannabis means breathing in smoke. This can result in a range of diseases, including bronchitis, heart disease, and cancer.

Cannabis smoke contains higher concentrations of cancer-causing chemicals than tobacco smoke. It also contains more **tar**. Medical studies have shown that smoking one cannabis cigarette deposits about four times more tar into the lungs than a filtered tobacco cigarette.

Recent studies show that the greatest number of pre-cancerous abnormalities (growths that will probably develop into cancer) appear in people who smoke cannabis and tobacco together.

Feeling unfit

Once people start smoking cannabis heavily, it changes the way they live. It's easy for cannabis smokers to fall into unhealthy habits – sleeping in late to recover from the night before, and eating irregular meals after late-night bingeing brought on by the **munchies**. Heavy cannabis smokers often develop coughs and other breathing disorders and become more vulnerable to colds and infections. So instead of feeling **high**, many cannabis users end up feeling pretty low!

Fertility and pregnancy

Cannabis smoking also has an effect on **fertility** (the ability to conceive children). Men with a history of heavy cannabis use tend to have reduced sperm counts, while women have irregular periods.

Smoking cannabis while pregnant can result in damage to the developing baby. Just like cigarette smokers, cannabis smokers deprive their unborn child of vital oxygen while they are smoking, and there is some evidence that heavy cannabis users give birth to low birth-weight babies.

Strokes

Some recent medical studies have suggested that there may be a link between smoking cannabis and **strokes**. When someone has a stroke, blood vessels in their brain are damaged, often causing part of their body to become **paralysed**. Some experts have suggested that smoking large amounts of cannabis in a short time helps to trigger damage to the blood vessels in the brain.

❚ Smoking cannabis has been recognized as a possible factor in causing strokes.

Mental health problems

Long-term cannabis users can also develop a range of mental health problems. They tend to suffer from **lethargy**, mood swings, and sleeplessness. Recent studies of heavy cannabis users have also shown that the mental effects of cannabis stay with them, even when they are no longer taking the drug. Several years later, these people are still suffering from short-term memory loss and problems in concentration and processing information.

■ Depression and other serious mental problems may be linked to heavy cannabis use.

Depression

Cannabis has the reputation of being a drug that makes the user happy, but it doesn't have a positive effect on everyone. Some people become withdrawn and depressed when they smoke cannabis.

There are many cases of young people who have become seriously depressed at a time when they were smoking cannabis heavily. It has not yet been proved that cannabis is directly responsible for the start of serious depression, but many experts believe there is a link.

Paranoia

Many cannabis smokers experience feelings of anxiety while they are under the influence of the drug (see pages 20–21). For the vast majority of people, these are only passing, if very frightening, experiences. However, for a few unlucky individuals, the feelings remain, and they develop serious **paranoia**. Paranoia is a crippling mental illness in which people may experience frequent **panic attacks**. Sufferers from paranoia often believe that people are following them, laughing at them, or plotting against them, and all of these feelings make it impossible for them to live a normal life.

Medical experts are not yet certain whether smoking cannabis can cause the development of paranoia. However, some researchers believe that for people who have a tendency to suffer from paranoia, cannabis may provide the trigger that tips them over the edge.

Schizophrenia

Two recent health studies have established a link between smoking cannabis and the very serious mental condition of **schizophrenia**. People with schizophrenia need intensive psychological care and drugs to help keep their condition under control. Experts are not certain whether cannabis directly causes schizophrenia, or whether it brings on the condition in people who were already at risk.

❙ If someone is experiencing worrying symptoms of mental illness, it's important for them to talk to a medically qualified person straightaway.

29

Losing out

When people smoke cannabis regularly, they miss out on a lot of good times. Some cannabis users get into a pattern of drifting from one **high** to the next – never doing anything positive in between. It's also very common for heavy cannabis users to lose their sense of energy and direction.

Drifting along

Many heavy cannabis users lose their enthusiasm for things they used to enjoy. Playing sports, going out dancing, or simply having fun with their friends can all take a back seat to getting high. Once they start on a regular cannabis habit, even the liveliest people can turn into boring "**dope heads**" whose idea of a great night out is sitting around smoking cannabis.

What's happened to my future?

Taking cannabis can do more than just ruin someone's fun. After smoking cannabis, people find it hard to take in new information, to concentrate on their work, or to remember what they've learnt. All these problems mean that cannabis users often do badly at school or college. Many get lower grades than they had hoped for, and some drop out of school or college altogether.

Joe's story

When Joe was sixteen his ambition was to study medicine, but then he got involved with a group of friends who all smoked cannabis heavily. He started taking days off school and just couldn't see the point of studying any more. He did badly in his exams and didn't get into medical college. At first, he didn't care too much. All he wanted was a job, and the chance to keep smoking cannabis with his friends. But none of his jobs led anywhere. Now he's 26 and working as a porter in the hospital where he had planned to do his training. Joe realizes he's thrown away his chance to do the one thing he really wanted to do.

▌Smoking cannabis often has the effect of cutting people off from their friends.

Just a short period of taking cannabis can affect a person's whole career – it may stop them from getting on the course that they were aiming for, or prevent them from passing some key exams. If people continue to smoke cannabis heavily, they may experience problems throughout their working lives. A significant number of people acknowledge the fact that their cannabis habit has prevented them from ever holding down a long-term job.

Serious consequences

Sometimes, smoking cannabis can lead to a crisis in a user's life. This may be a personal problem, or it can be very public. When someone in the public eye is caught with the drug, it can have serious consequences for their career.

❚ Relationships can turn sour when one member of a couple feels that their partner is smoking too much cannabis.

Breaking up

Sometimes, cannabis can be the cause of relationship problems, as a girlfriend or boyfriend decides that they've had enough of their partner's habit. When someone decides that they no longer want to live with a "**dope head**", things can go two ways. Sometimes the cannabis user decides to give up the drug. But in other cases, the user makes the choice to stay with their drug – and has to face the fact that their cannabis habit has led to the breakdown of their relationship.

Athletes in trouble

Athletes who take cannabis run the risk of being excluded from their sport. In 2003, US snowboarding star Tara Zwink tested positive for cannabis and was given a two-year ban from international competitions. Another snowboarder, Canadian Ross Rebagliati, who also had a positive cannabis test, has been banned from travel to the United States unless he receives special permission from the government.

The end of a career

Although cannabis is seen as relatively harmless compared with hard drugs such as heroin or cocaine, it is still an illegal substance. So when a celebrity is connected with cannabis it can mean the end of their career. This is particularly true when that celebrity is supposed to be a role model for young people. Several presenters on youth TV shows have said goodbye to their careers after they confessed to smoking cannabis.

A hip-hop star's story

In March 2004, the hip-hop band Big Brovaz sacked band member Flawless after he was caught carrying cannabis through customs at a US airport. Flawless was searched, arrested, and sent back home. Band member Randy said: "Big Brovaz were in a state of shock and felt Flawless had let the side down." Flawless told a reporter: "I'm very sorry for this stupid behaviour, I put everyone's careers at stake. I hope they will forgive me."

❚ A photo of Big Brovaz taken before Flawless's cannabis habit put an end to his career with the band. Flawless is on the far right.

A gateway drug?

Many people believe that cannabis is a **gateway drug** that can lead on to hard drugs such as heroin and cocaine. These people claim that once a person has tried smoking cannabis, it's very tempting for them to move on to something stronger.

Is there a link?

People who support the "gateway" argument point to the figures for hard drug users, which show that almost all of them started out by smoking cannabis at a young age. However, others argue that the kinds of people who take hard drugs are very likely to try cannabis too.

Playing safe

Most of the evidence seems to point to the fact that the vast majority of cannabis users never move on to harder drugs. A recent UK survey revealed that 60 per cent of young people aged between 20 and 24 had used cannabis, but only 1 per cent had used harder drugs. It seems that most people recognize that the risks and penalties of taking hard drugs are just much too high.

I Rock star Ozzy Osbourne is one of many high-profile figures who moved from cannabis on to hard drugs. Ozzy's son, Jack, has said publicly that he believes that cannabis is a gateway drug.

Dangerous dealers

There is also another way in which taking cannabis may lead to experiments with harder drugs. Using cannabis puts people in touch with drug **dealers**, who usually sell a range of different drugs. Often, these dealers are only too keen to persuade their customers to buy harder and more expensive drugs. Some dealers even add crack cocaine or heroin to cannabis **joints** so that the smoker becomes dependent on these drugs.

Many people believe that drug dealers provide a very dangerous link between cannabis and hard drugs. Some of them even argue that cannabis should be **decriminalized** and made legal for people to use in small quantities, so that it is taken out of the hands of the dealers. However, many others strongly oppose this idea (see also pages 46–47).

❙ Many cannabis users get their drug from dealers, who may also offer them a range of hard drugs.

ViewpoiNTS

Many people get involved in the debate over whether cannabis is a gateway drug, and there are some powerful arguments on both sides.

- ### Cannabis leads to harder drugs
  Once people have started using cannabis, they may be tempted to experiment with other drugs. They may be given other drugs, mixed into the cannabis. They may also be persuaded by dealers to try hard drugs such as heroin.

- ### Cannabis is not a gateway drug
  Most cannabis users never move on to harder drugs. They realize that taking hard drugs is very risky and that the penalties for using them are extremely harsh. Also, many users never meet a dealer, because they get their supplies from friends or acquaintances.

  What do you think?

An ancient cure

Cannabis has been used as a medicine for thousands of years, but by the 1930s it was banned in most countries. Today, some people use cannabis illegally to treat a range of medical complaints, but others think that taking cannabis is just too risky.

Giving relief

In most countries, cannabis is banned as a legal medicine. However, some people take the drug illegally to help combat the symptoms of a range of illnesses and disorders. People report that cannabis helps with the pain associated with **multiple sclerosis** and the shakes produced by **Parkinson's disease**. Cannabis also seems to have the effect of reducing painful pressure in the eyes of **glaucoma** sufferers. The drug may reduce the headaches and nausea that many people experience during chemotherapy (the chemical therapy used for treating cancer). Some people claim that cannabis is more effective than other medical drugs in combating pain and nausea because it helps patients to relax.

❙ Some people say that cannabis can help to relax the muscle stiffness and cramps associated with multiple sclerosis.

▌ This scientist is conducting research into the effects of cannabis. Many people feel that more work needs to be done before it is safe to use cannabis as a medicine.

Unknown dangers

Many people worry that taking cannabis can have negative health effects – especially when the user is already ill. They say that not enough research has been done into the **side effects** of cannabis, or into the way that it might react with other drugs. They also point out that cannabis smoke contains hundreds of chemicals – many of which have never been tested for their effects on the human body.

There are also many risks in taking a drug that comes in unknown strengths, is exempt from any quality control, and is not given in doses recommended by a doctor. Opponents of cannabis use argue that although cannabis appears to have some beneficial effects, more medical studies need to be undertaken.

Room for change?

Should cannabis be made legal for medical use? Lots of different people get involved in this debate. Some patients and their supporters campaign hard for cannabis to be **decriminalized**, so they can use it without breaking the law. There are also some doctors who would like to **prescribe** cannabis as a medical drug. Medicinal cannabis could be prescribed in limited doses and in non-smokable form – possibly as tablets, sprays, or skin patches. However, critics suggest that patients may misuse these drugs, using them to get **high**, instead of restricting them to purely medical purposes. You can read more about these arguments on pages 46–47.

The cannabis business

Cannabis is big business. A few powerful people, often known as **drug barons**, control the growing of cannabis and organize the drug's illegal **import** into other countries. Cannabis **traffickers** use a range of methods to smuggle huge quantities of the drug past border police and officials and into the hands of the **dealers**.

Growing cannabis

Most cannabis is grown in remote areas of South and Central America, North Africa, and South-East Asia. Many of these regions have **economic** problems, and their governments have little money to spend on controlling the growing of cannabis. Often, a government is too poor to clamp down on the drug barons, or is too busy with other problems. However, in some cases, members of the government are themselves involved in the drug business.

Dangerous links

In many cases, the people in charge of growing and smuggling cannabis are also involved in criminal activities or terrorist organizations. Recent surveys have shown that all the major terrorist groups in Central and South America are funded by money from cannabis. All too often, violence and drug trafficking go hand in hand. But how many people think, when they buy a bag of cannabis, that they are helping to finance violence and crime?

"By refusing to buy illicit drugs people are refusing to support international terror."

Partnership for a Drug-Free America, an organization dedicated to helping young people reject drug abuse

Other sources

In recent years, cannabis has been grown in new ways and in new areas. Growers in the Netherlands, where cannabis production is not illegal, have developed methods for growing cannabis in greenhouses. Some Dutch companies openly advertise cannabis seeds for sale and **export**, and Dutch growing methods have been widely copied. There are now illegal greenhouses hidden away in many areas of Europe and the United States.

Because cannabis seeds and seedlings are so easily available, some users choose to grow their own plants secretly. These people may grow cannabis plants in a cupboard or a wardrobe or even out of doors. Some secret cannabis growers sell the drug to their friends or even start up small illegal businesses to supply the drug to other users. However, people who grow cannabis risk being detected by drug agencies and face heavy fines and imprisonment.

❙ In the Netherlands, cannabis plants are grown in vast greenhouses.

❗ For the people at the top of the cannabis business, there are huge profits to be made. An Australian survey found that the total amount spent on cannabis in 1999 was twice as much as that spent on wine.

Smuggling cannabis

Once the leaves and flowers of the cannabis plant have been harvested, they are dried and packed into bundles ready for **export**. These bundles are quite bulky, so **traffickers** have to find some very ingenious ways of hiding them. The most common way to smuggle cannabis overland is inside small commercial or private vehicles. Here, bundles of the drug are hidden inside false compartments, fuel tanks, seats, and even tyres. Larger quantities of cannabis are often carried in trucks with a false compartment or disguised amongst a load of bulky goods.

Shipments of cannabis also arrive by sea, hidden in large cargo vessels. Ships and boats carrying cannabis generally avoid busy shipping lanes and head for more remote waters, where the cannabis is off-loaded onto smaller boats. Small pleasure boats and fishing boats are also used to deliver the drug to secret drop-off points.

Cannabis dealing

Illegal loads of cannabis are usually kept in a secret depot. The drug is then sold on to **dealers**. Some drug dealers sell a range of drugs including cannabis, but others simply deal in cannabis, preferring not to get involved with hard drugs such as heroin. As with all illegal drug dealing networks, the people at the top of the network keep most of the profits, while the dealers on the streets face the greatest risk of being discovered.

Most cannabis dealers are heavy cannabis users themselves, so they are grateful to receive a free supply of the drug as part or all of their payment. These dealers are very keen to find new users who will help to pay to support their habit – and one of the easiest groups to target is the young.

Dealers hang around places where young people gather, such as games arcades, swimming pools, and rock concerts. Sometimes they even wait outside schools and colleges. Often a dealer will make contact with some young cannabis users and rely on them to bring in new customers.

▌Cannabis smuggling can involve huge sums of money. The cannabis found hidden in this shipping container was worth more than £600,000 (US$1,000,000).

Tackling cannabis distribution

The drug prevention agencies are up against some extremely sharp operators. In 2000, US drug squads managed to crack a huge cannabis distribution ring that was using the US postal system to disguise its massive country-wide operation. The drugs ring used the trucks, planes, and facilities of a major mail company to carry tons of cannabis from Mexico to cities throughout the United States. More than a hundred people were charged with drug-trafficking offences.

Cannabis and the law

What should the law do about cannabis and what is the best way to deal with offenders? Governments have tackled these questions in different ways.

UK laws

In the United Kingdom, the law has recently been changed, and cannabis has been reclassified as a Class C drug, rather than a Class B drug like **amphetamines** (speed). However, cannabis is still illegal. If someone is caught using or possessing cannabis they can be given a formal **caution**, which is entered on police records. Depending on the amount found, and on whether the person already has a caution, they may be charged, fined, and sent to prison for up to two years. People caught supplying cannabis can be sent to prison for up to fourteen years, and be given an unlimited fine.

▋ In the United States, people possessing cannabis run the risk of being arrested and sent to jail.

The Australian approach

Australia has different laws for different states. In South Australia, Australian Capital Territory, and the Northern Territory, possession and growing of small quantities of cannabis has been **decriminalized**. This means that offenders pay a fine but no conviction is recorded. In Victoria, first-time minor cannabis users are cautioned and referred to a drug education service. Australian **federal law** against people smuggling cannabis into the country is much harsher than in the individual states. Anyone caught arriving in Australia carrying cannabis can face a fine of up to Aus$250,000 (£100,000) and up to ten years in prison.

A tough line

In the United States, drug laws and penalties vary from state to state. However, all US states impose heavy penalties on anyone involved with drugs. One of the toughest US states on drugs use is Texas, where the penalty for possessing a small amount of cannabis is up to 180 days in prison and/or a fine of US$2,000 (£1,000).

Viewpoints

People disagree about the best way to stop people from using cannabis.

- ## Cannabis users should be punished heavily

The best way to stop people taking drugs is to scare them. If people realize that they could lose a large amount of money or be sent to jail for using cannabis, they are more likely to stay away from the drug.

- ## Punishing cannabis users is a waste of valuable resources

It's a waste of money and time to prosecute cannabis users, when the police and the courts should be concentrating on catching drug **dealers** and smugglers instead. Sending people to prison for smoking cannabis puts an extra burden on already overcrowded prisons. While they are in prison, these minor drug offenders mix with violent criminals as well as people who use hard drugs. They may end up with a serious drug habit and be introduced to a life of crime.

What do you think?

I A tourist buys cannabis in one of Amsterdam's "brown cafes". Cafes like this have a special licence to sell limited amounts of cannabis to people over eighteen.

A different approach

While the United States takes a very tough line on cannabis users, other countries have tackled their drugs problem in a different way. In particular, the Dutch government has relaxed its laws on cannabis use, whilst keeping strict control on hard drugs such as heroin. What are the reasons behind this policy and does the Dutch approach really work?

Decriminalizing cannabis

In the Netherlands, the Dutch government has taken the decision to **decriminalize** cannabis. This means that it is not against the law to possess small quantities of the drug for personal use. Cannabis is sold in special shops that have a licence to sell restricted amounts to people over eighteen. However, the storing of large quantities of cannabis for **dealing** on the streets has remained illegal.

Question

What's the difference between a drug that's decriminalized and one that's legal?

Why decriminalize cannabis?

Supporters of the Dutch approach say that if cannabis is decriminalized it can be supplied more safely. They claim that when cannabis is decriminalized, users can buy the drug without having any contact with dealers, who may try to sell them harder drugs. They also say that without the task of policing cannabis use, the Dutch police have more time to concentrate on the dealers in harder drugs.

A dangerous step?

Opponents of this approach say that decriminalization sends out the wrong message and encourages cannabis use. Cannabis has many well-recognized harmful effects. So should a government encourage the sale of a product that is known to be harmful? Also, while drug dealers no longer sell cannabis in the Netherlands, the dealers have not disappeared from the country's city streets. Since the decriminalization of cannabis in the Netherlands, the Dutch capital Amsterdam has become a world centre for drug dealing.

What's the evidence?

The evidence on drug taking in the Netherlands is difficult to interpret. The country has not seen a dramatic increase in cannabis use amongst its own population. However, the number of drug **addicts** in Amsterdam is very high. This can be partly explained by the fact that the liberal approach to cannabis in the Netherlands has made it into a centre for drug taking, and many addicts have chosen to make Amsterdam their home.

❚ Cannabis seeds for sale in an Amsterdam shop. Not everyone in the Netherlands thinks this is a good idea.

Answer

A decriminalized drug can only be purchased in small amounts and must be kept for strictly personal use. A legal drug, such as tobacco or alcohol, can be purchased in large quantities and offered to others of legal age.

Should the law be changed?

In countries where cannabis use is illegal, some people campaign strongly for a change in the law. But not everyone who campaigns for change wants the same thing. What are the arguments for changing the law, and would any of these changes be a good thing?

Different arguments

People have a range of different views about how the laws on cannabis should be relaxed. Some people support the total **decriminalization** of cannabis, using the same arguments as the Dutch government (see pages 44–45). A much smaller group of people say that the drug should be **legalized**, and treated just like alcohol or tobacco. They say that alcohol and tobacco cause more dangers to health, are more **addictive**, and have a much stronger link with violence than cannabis. They question why these drugs are legal while cannabis is banned. There is also a significant group of people who campaign for the partial decriminalization of cannabis, so that it can be used for medical purposes.

A valuable medicine?

Some people claim that cannabis offers them relief from pain and suffering (see pages 36–37). They suggest that cannabis should be partially decriminalized so that it is no longer against the law for the drug to be used for medical purposes.

❚ Some people feel so strongly that cannabis should be decriminalized that they go on marches to promote their point of view.

Some doctors also support the partial decriminalization of cannabis. They say that they would like to have the opportunity to **prescribe** it to certain patients – especially those suffering from the painful muscle cramps caused by **multiple sclerosis**. However, many other doctors argue that this is not necessary. They say that there are other legal drugs that could have the same effect.

Too many risks

However, many people think that cannabis should remain illegal. They are concerned about the drug's effects on health – both in the short term and the long term. They point out the dangers of lung disease and cancer, and the very worrying link with serious mental illnesses such as **paranoia**, depression, and **schizophrenia**. They also point to the drug's **demotivating** effects, causing many young people to throw away their chances of a rewarding future.

In particular, many people are worried that not enough is known about the ways that cannabis can affect the body and mind. They believe that it is dangerous and wrong to make a drug easily available before more is known about it, and when it has the potential to damage lives.

▌For many people, the health dangers caused by cannabis add up to a powerful argument against ever using the drug.

Cannabis and schools

Most young people do not take drugs, but some teenagers feel that they want to give cannabis a try. Teenagers today are under many pressures and some may feel tempted to turn to drugs. What should be done when cannabis use gets out of hand at school? Some schools have decided that their only option is to take a very hard line against illegal drug use.

A growing problem

Many teachers and parents are becoming increasingly worried about the problem of drugs in schools. Because so many young people are all gathered together in one place, it's easy for a

▐ Most schools manage to keep drug use under control, so pupils can enjoy learning and socializing with their friends.

cannabis habit to spread through a school. Of course, not all schools are badly affected by drugs. However, once a school has a serious drugs problem, it can become a target for drug **dealers**. With these problems in mind, many schools have decided to impose heavy penalties on any pupil who is found in possession of, or using, cannabis or other drugs.

Zero tolerance

Many schools have adopted a policy of "zero tolerance" towards cannabis and other drugs. This means that any pupil who is caught using cannabis, or with cannabis in their possession, is automatically punished. In some schools, a pupil is first given a warning, or they may be suspended for a short time. However, in other schools, pupils may be expelled immediately. In some US schools, pupils who are caught with cannabis can be prevented from graduating from high school, which means they are unable to go on to college or university.

Viewpoints

Not everyone agrees that a zero tolerance approach is the right way to deal with a cannabis problem in schools.

- ## Schools should take a hard line on cannabis

Cannabis use is a major problem for the students and their schools, because it stops them from functioning properly. Schools need to take very firm action to stop the problem of cannabis use from spreading. Students who choose not to take drugs should not have to suffer because of other pupils' choices. Schools need to set a clear example to all their students that taking cannabis is never acceptable.

- ## Zero tolerance is not the answer

Punishing students by depriving them of their education is not the way to solve the problem. Pupils who are expelled may become more rebellious, and may be more at risk from problems with drugs. A better approach would be to provide the students with **counselling** and education about drugs, while allowing them to stay in school as long as they are drug free.

What do you think?

Help and advice

Are there things that worry you about cannabis? If there are – either now or in the future – there are lots of people and places to contact. There are many organizations that offer help and advice on cannabis and cannabis-related problems. You can find more information about these organizations on pages 54–55 of this book.

Finding out more

If you want to find out more about cannabis and the problems associated with it, you can start by contacting the organizations listed at the back of this book. Many of them have useful websites and some supply information packs. Some organizations have local branches, and they will also provide helpful links to people you can contact.

Someone to talk to

Sometimes it can be hard to talk to people you know about the things that are worrying you. You may want to discuss your concerns **in confidence**, knowing that whatever you say won't be passed on to anyone you know. You may also feel that you need some expert advice.

Fortunately, there's an easy way to find somebody sympathetic to talk to. Several organizations have telephone helplines – phones that are staffed by specially trained advisers. These advisers will listen carefully to your concerns and questions and offer you advice and support. Some helplines are open 24 hours a day, which means you can call them at any time – even if you have a problem in the middle of the night.

It's up to you

Are you worried that some time in the future you might be offered cannabis – and even be tempted to say yes? Here are some things you can do to put yourself less at risk:

■ Be prepared. Think over what you'll say in advance if you are offered cannabis.

■ Think hard about the consequences and risks of taking cannabis. Is this really what you want to do?

- Remember that you're not alone. There are telephone numbers to call and people you can talk to about your worries.

- Most of all, remember – it's your life. Nobody else can tell you what to do. It's up to you to make your own decisions.

"Lots of people say that cannabis is harmless, but that's not how it was for me. It made me miss out on all sorts of things – and I got really depressed. I don't know whether smoking grass is the reason for my depression, but it certainly hasn't helped. Let me tell you, it just isn't worth it."

Scott, an ex-cannabis smoker who started taking cannabis in his early teens

▌ It's up to you to choose how you want to live. Do you really think that taking drugs is the best way to make the most of your life?

Glossary

addiction when a person is dependent on (unable to manage without) a drug and finds it extremely hard to stop using it

amphetamine type of stimulant drug that speeds up the activity of the brain

bong type of water-filled pipe used for smoking cannabis. The water in the bong cools down the cannabis smoke.

cannabis psychosis strong feelings of panic and anxiety that are caused by taking cannabis

caution warning not to do something

concentrated very strong

counselling advice and guidance given to people to help resolve their problems

crave to have a powerful longing for something

dealer person who buys and sells drugs illegally

decriminalize to change the law so that something is no longer illegal under certain circumstances

demotivate to stop someone from wanting to do or achieve things

dope head slang name for someone who smokes a lot of cannabis

drug baron someone who controls the growing, smuggling, and selling of drugs

economic to do with earning and using money

export to send goods to another country for sale

federal law law for a country, such as Australia or the United States, that is made up of a number of states. Federal law is often different from state law.

fertility ability to create babies

gateway drug any drug that has the effect of making its user want to take more powerful drugs

glaucoma eye disease in which pressure inside the eyeball causes the sufferer to lose their vision and even become blind

hash hardened sap from the cannabis plant. Hash is short for hashish.

hemp long, stringy fibres from the stems of the cannabis plant. Hemp is often made into ropes.

high feeling of happiness and relaxation

hippy someone who chooses not to live like most other people. Hippies often live together in groups.

import to bring goods from abroad into a country

in confidence privately, without telling anyone else

inhibition feeling or fear that holds someone back from expressing their feelings or stops them from behaving naturally

intoxicating causing someone to lose complete control of their body and mind

joint cannabis cigarette

leaf cannabis dried cannabis made from the leaves of the cannabis plant

legalize to allow something by law

lethargy lack of energy and enthusiasm

multiple sclerosis disease that causes loss of movement and feeling in parts of the body

munchies slang name for the powerful feelings of hunger that people experience a couple of hours after taking cannabis

nicotine addictive drug found in all tobacco products

panic attack sudden very strong feeling of anxiety, which makes a person's heart race

paralysed unable to move

paranoia mental condition involving feelings of suspicion and distrust – a sense that everyone is out to get you, or to criticize your behaviour or actions

Parkinson's disease disease that makes a person shake uncontrollably

prescribe to write an instruction (a prescription) that authorizes a medicine to be issued to a patient

psychological dependence when a person feels they need drugs to get through everyday life and cannot cope without them

Rastafarian follower of Rastafarianism, a religion that was started in Jamaica in the 1930s

receptor part of the brain that responds to a chemical stimulus and sends messages throughout the body

resin hardened sap (the juice inside plants)

schizophrenia serious mental disorder that can lead to confused thinking and changes in a person's personality and behaviour

side effect unwanted effect of a drug or medical treatment

solvent type of liquid that makes another substance dissolve

spliff slang name for a cannabis cigarette

stoned strongly affected by drugs or alcohol

stroke damage to part of the brain, which may cause part of the body to be paralyzed

tar harmful, brown sticky substance that is found in tobacco and cannabis smoke

THC very powerful chemical in cannabis that reacts with parts of the brain. The initials THC stand for delta-9-tetrahydrocannabinol.

tolerance need for larger and larger doses of a drug to get the same effect

trafficker person who smuggles or transports drugs, usually in large amounts and across the borders of different countries

uncoordinated not properly controlled

withdrawal symptoms unpleasant physical and mental feelings experienced during the process of giving up an addictive drug

Contacts and further information

There are a number of organizations that provide information and advice about cannabis. Some have helpful websites, or provide information packs and leaflets, while others offer help and support over the phone.

Contacts in the UK

Adfam
Waterbridge House, 32–36 Loman Street, London SE1 0EH
Tel: 020 7928 8898
www.adfam.org.uk
Adfam is a national charity that gives confidential support and information to families and friends of drug users. They also run family support groups around the UK.

Connexions Direct
Helpline: 080 800 13219
(8 a.m.–2 a.m. daily)
Text: 07766 4 13219
www.connexions-direct.com
This service for young people aged thirteen to nineteen offers information and advice on a wide range of topics, including drugs.

DrugScope
32–36 Loman Street, London SE1 0EE
Tel: 020 7928 1211
www.drugscope.org.uk
A national drugs information agency with services that include a library, a wide range of publications, and a website with drug factsheets.

Families Anonymous
Doddington & Rollo Community Association, Charlotte Despard Avenue, Battersea, London SW11 5HD
Helpline: 0845 1200 660
www.famanon.org.uk
An organization involved in support groups for parents and families of drug users. They can put you in touch with groups in different parts of the country.

FRANK
Tel: 0800 776600
Email: frank@talktofrank.com
www.talktofrank.com
An organization for young people that gives free, confidential advice and information about drugs, 24 hours a day.

Marijuana Anonymous (MA)
Tel: 07940 503438
www.marijuana-anonymous.org
An organization run by people who used to be dependent on cannabis, dedicated to helping others to recover from their addiction.

Marijuana Anonymous Online
www.ma-online.org
A Marijuana Anonymous website with a chatspace for people with cannabis problems.

Narcotics Anonymous
UK Service Office, 202 City Road, London EC1V 2PH
Helpline: 020 7730 0009
(10 a.m.–10 p.m. daily)
www.ukna.org
Narcotics Anonymous is run mainly by people who have a history of drug problems. They have a helpline for users and their friends and relatives, plus meetings throughout the UK.

Release
Helpline: 0845 4500 215
(10 a.m.–5.30 p.m. Mon–Fri)
Email: ask@release.org.uk
www.release.org.uk
An organization that provides legal advice to drug users, their families, and friends. The advice is free, professional, non-judgemental, and confidential.

Contacts in Australia and New Zealand

Alcohol & Other Drugs Council of Australia (ADCA)
17 Napier Close, Deakin, ACT 2600
Tel: 02 6281 1002
www.adca.org.au
ADCA works to prevent or reduce the harm caused by drugs.

Australian Drug Foundation
409 King Street, West Melbourne, VIC 3003
Tel: 03 9278 8100
www.adf.org.au
An organization that works to prevent and reduce drug problems.

The DARE (Drug Abuse Resistance Education) Foundation of New Zealand
PO Box 50744, Porirua, New Zealand
Tel: 04 238 9550
www.dare.org.nz
An organization that provides drug prevention education programmes.

Foundation for Alcohol and Drug Education (FADE)
9 Anzac Street, PO Box 33–1505, Takapuna, Auckland, New Zealand
Tel: 09 489 1719
www.fade.org.nz
A national organization that provides services throughout New Zealand.

Marijuana Anonymous Australia
PO Box 2002, Hindmarsh 5007
South Australia
Tel: 618 834 08989
www.geocities.com/maaustralia/
The Australian branch of Marijuana Anonymous.

Narcotics Anonymous
Australian Service Office, 1st Floor, 204 King Street, Newtown, NSW 2042
National helpline: 1300 652 820
http://na.org.au/
The Australian division of Narcotics Anonymous.

Turning Point
54–62 Gertrude Street, Fitzroy, VIC 3065
Helpline (DirectLine): 1800 888 236
www.turningpoint.org.au
Turning Point provides support services to people affected by drugs.

Further reading

Dr Miriam Stoppard's Drug Information File: From Alcohol and Tobacco to Ecstasy and Heroin, by Miriam Stoppard (Dorling Kindersley, 1999)

Drugs and You, by Bridget Lawless (Heinemann Library, 2000)

Drugs: The Truth, by Aidan Macfarlane and Ann McPherson (Oxford University Press, 2003)

Health Issues: Drugs, by Sarah Lennard-Brown (Hodder Children's Books, 2004)

Need to Know: Cannabis, by Sean Connolly (Heinemann Library, 2002)

Teen Issues: Drugs, by Joanna Watson and Joanna Kedge (Raintree, 2004)

Why Do People Take Drugs?, by Patsy Westcott (Hodder Children's Books, 2000)

Wise Guides: Drugs, by Anita Naik (Hodder Children's Books, 1997)

Further research

If you want to find out more about problems related to cannabis, you can search the Internet, using a search engine such as Google. Try using keywords such as:

Cannabis + law
Cannabis + medicine
Cannabis + decriminalization
Cannabis dependence
Cannabis + depression
Cannabis + schizophrenia

Index

addiction 22, 45, 46; *see also* psychological dependence
alcohol 9, 13, 15, 21, 46
anxiety 10, 13, 20, 21, 28
athletes 16, 32
Australia 39, 43

babies 26, 27
Big Brovaz 33
blunts 8
bong 8
brain 10–11, 12, 27; *see also* memory; mental health problems
breathing problems 26, 27

cancer 11, 26, 27, 36, 47
cannabis plant 6, 8, 38–39
cannabis psychosis 20
careers 16, 30, 31, 32–33, 47
celebrities 16, 32, 33, 34
cocaine 33, 34, 35
concentration 12, 18, 19, 26, 28, 30
counselling 49
cramps 7, 36, 47
cravings 22, 23

dealers 9, 17, 35, 38, 40, 43, 44, 49
decriminalization 35, 37, 43, 44–45, 46–47
dependence 22, 23
depression 10, 13, 23, 28, 47, 51
dizziness 13, 21
"dope heads" 30, 32
driving 18
drug barons 5, 38

education 43, 49; *see also* schools
effects of use 5, 9, 10–13, 18–19, 45
    long-term 26–27, 28, 30–31, 47
    mental 5, 19, 26, 28–29; *see also* mental health problems
    physical 18, 22
    short-term 18–19, 47
energy 16, 19, 25, 26, 30

fear 10, 21
fertility 27

friends 17, 18, 21, 25, 30, 31, 48

"ganja" 9, 15
gateway drug(s) 4–5, 34–35
giving up 22, 23, 24–25
government action 5, 7, 38, 41

happiness 10, 13
hash 9, 14
hash oil 8, 9
health problems 11, 26–29, 37, 47
heart 10, 21, 26
help 24, 50–51, 54–55
hemp 6, 7
heroin 5, 33, 34, 35, 40
hippies 14
history of cannabis 6–7

information 50, 54–55
irritability 13, 21, 25

joint(s) 8, 9, 16, 24, 35

law 5, 7, 42–43, 46–47
leaf cannabis 8, 9
lethargy 19, 28

Marijuana Anonymous 24
Marley, Bob 16
medicinal uses 7, 14, 15, 36–37, 46–47
memory 11, 19, 26, 30
mental health problems 5, 26, 28–29, 47
moods 10, 12, 13, 23, 28
multiple sclerosis 15, 36, 47
munchies 12, 13, 27

names for cannabis 9
nausea 21, 25
Netherlands 39, 44–45
New Zealand 29
nicotine *see* tobacco

Osbourne, Jack 34
Osbourne, Ozzy 34

pain relief 7, 15, 36
panic attacks 10, 13, 20, 21, 24, 29
paranoia 13, 20, 21, 24, 28–29, 47
Parkinson's disease 15, 36

penalties 42–43, 48
pregnancy 27
prison 42, 43
psychological dependence 22, 23
psychosis 20

Rastafarianism 14, 15, 16
relationships 4, 24, 32
relaxation 12, 17, 22, 36
research 11, 26, 29, 37
resin 8, 9
risk taking 18, 19
rock musicians 16, 33, 34

schizophrenia 29, 47
school(s) 4, 19, 30, 40, 48–49; *see also* education
senses 10, 12
side effects 20–21, 37; *see also* health problems; mental health problems
"skunk" 8
sleep 25, 27, 28
smuggling 38, 39, 40–41, 43
South America 38, 39
speech 12, 18
"spinning out" 21
spliffs 9, 18
sport 16, 30, 32
strength 8, 9, 20, 37
strokes 27

tar 26
telephone helplines 50, 54–55
terrorism 39
Thailand 7
THC 10
tobacco 8, 9, 11, 22, 23, 26, 27, 46
tolerance 22
trade, cannabis 5, 38–39, 40–41
traffickers *see* smuggling
treatment 22

United Kingdom 42
United States 7, 15, 22, 27, 32, 39, 41, 42, 43, 49

vomiting 13, 21

withdrawal symptoms 25

zero tolerance 49